PEOPLE AT WORK
in
INDIA

ISABELLE DAUDY AND JOHN OGLE

B.T. BATSFORD LTD   LONDON

CONTENTS

Frontispiece
Shopping at an Indian market.

Typeset by Tek-Art Ltd, Kent
and printed and bound in Great Britain by
Richard Clay Ltd
Chichester, Sussex
for the publishers
B.T. Batsford Ltd
4 Fitzhardinge Street
London W1H 0AH

ISBN 0 7134 5157 2

INTRODUCTION

"India is large, very large, and not at all easy to understand."
(Indira Gandhi, Prime Minister of India, 1966 to 1977, and 1980 to 1984)

India is a country of extremes: it contains the world's highest mountain range (the Himalayas) in the north, as well as one of the world's largest deserts (the Rajosthan Desert) in the north-west, and some of the most fertile agricultural plains in the north-east and south-east. Since it

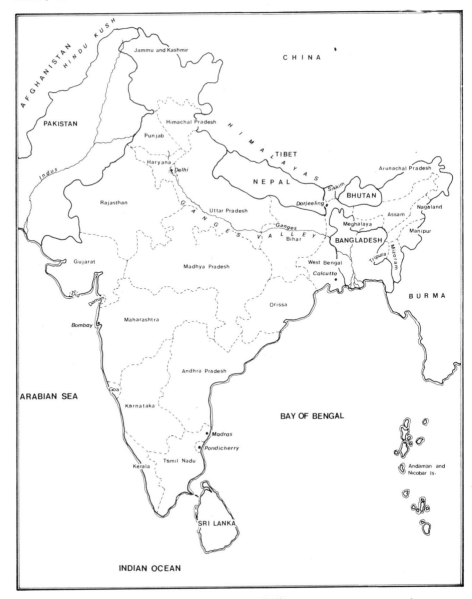

Buses and trains often get so crowded that the passengers climb on to the roofs and hang out of doors and windows to stay on.

gained independence from the British in 1947, India's population has more than doubled, making it one of the most densely populated countries in the world: one-sixth of mankind on one-fortieth of the land. With about 700 million people, it has become the world's largest democracy – and its population continues to grow at a rate of more than a million a month. Indian cities are crammed with people. They squeeze into buses, hang out of windows and climb on to the roofs, trying to get to work on time. Whole families live and work on the pavements. Even in the countryside it is rare to see a deserted road – everywhere there are people, working, eating, sleeping.

India's many different races range from the Aryan, who are tall with lighter skin and hair, to the Mongoloid who are stocky, with a brown complexion, high cheek-bones and widely-spaced eyes, and the Australoid who are short, with very black skin, wide faces and broad noses. Indians do not even all speak the same language. Although Hindi and English are spoken by a small, educated and powerful group throughout the country, the vast

majority of people only know their own local language, and – perhaps – an even more localized dialect. There are 5 official languages in the country, each with its own script, and about 150 which are less widely spoken. Many hundreds of local dialects have no written form at all and are only spoken in one or two villages.

Different areas also have distinctive ways of dressing, different food, different customs and festivals, different industries and different crops. For instance, in the northern desert state of Rajasthan, the men wear bright turbans and a white cloth (called a *dhoti*) wrapped round their legs. The women have long, pleated skirts with embroidered blouses and a large veil which they tuck into their skirts and wear over their heads. There is little farming because the soil is poor, and people mainly survive by herding sheep, goats and camels, by trading, and by making some of the country's loveliest handicrafts. Men often live in dwellings apart from the women, and in many villages the women are still kept in strict seclusion, only rarely going outside their own courtyards. When they do go out, most rural Rajasthani women cover

Apart from the typically Indian sari which she is wearing, this woman looks as if she could be African. She has very dark skin, broad features and thick lips.

their faces with their veils.

In the south, men are usually bare-headed and wear a coloured cloth called a *lunghi* which they tie round their stomach like a skirt. Women wear *saris*, which are long pieces of cloth tucked into a petticoat in graceful folds and gathered across the breasts and over the left shoulder. In the more fertile areas, most men and women work in the fields producing crops such as banana, rice, cotton and sugar-cane. Some people keep goats and cattle, but there are no camels in this part of India. Men and women live together, and women are commonly seen in public, shopping or working with their faces uncovered.

In spite of this variety, some aspects of the country's geography and social structure have given India the sense of being one nation. From earliest times, different parts of the subcontinent have been colonized by migrating peoples from all over the world (which is why there are still so many racial types today). Most of these outsiders came into India through the north-western frontier. But on every other side, India was well-insulated from invaders. To the north it was protected by the towering Himalayas, to the east by thick jungle, and on the other two sides of the subcontinent's triangle, by the huge expanses of the Indian Ocean. In the sixteenth and seventeenth centuries the ocean began to be opened up to the world by trading ships, but by this time India had developed a strong and distinctive culture which was able to absorb outside influences.

The origins of modern Indian culture can be traced to about 1750 years before Christ, when a group of people called the Aryans began to enter India from the Hindu Kush (see map, p. 3). The penetration of these Aryans took place over several centuries, during which time many waves of migrants went deeper and deeper into the Indus and Ganges valleys. We still know very little about what happened so long ago, but it is probable that before the Aryan invasions most of India's inhabitants were the dark-skinned Dravidians, ancestors of present-day South Indians.

During the first few centuries of Aryan migration, society was much less rigidly structured than it later became. It was probably divided into three broad social classes: the warriors or aristocracy, the priests, and the common people. It was still possible, during this period, for an ordinary person to do well and to join one of the higher classes.

The native Dravidians were feared and despised by the migrants (who often had to fight them for control of an area), and they were considered to be outside Aryan society. Slowly the Aryans gave up their nomadic, wandering habits and began to evolve an increasingly hierarchical and rigid society. Different classes of people (with the darker natives still treated as the lowest) became fixed social groups or "castes" who could only marry among themselves. It became increasingly difficult – and eventually impossible – for members of one caste to enter into another, higher caste. Sometimes it was possible for an entire caste to gain a better position in society, but this process usually took more than one generation.

Different castes increasingly specialized in certain areas of work, and were assigned a well-defined rank in the local society. This rank depended on the kind of work which it became traditional for the members of a caste to do. According to the Aryan religion (which later became known as Hinduism, and which more than 80 per cent of Indians still follow today) some kinds of work – such as cleaning toilets or making leather shoes – were considered "polluting", while other kinds – such as teaching or trading – were considered "pure". The more polluting was your caste's occupation, the lower was your rank in society. Some castes were considered so polluted that higher castes were not even allowed to touch them, because they were afraid of becoming polluted themselves. People from these lower castes were called Untouchables. This system often led to terrible inequalities, and oppression of the weaker castes. But, because toilet-cleaners and shoe-makers were as necessary to Hindu society as teachers or merchants, different castes had to rely on each other. In a village, higher castes were expected to help and protect the lower castes in times of need, and the lower castes were expected to provide faithful service in return.

This classic "caste system" was broadly established about 1000 years ago, and has spread and survived, with few changes, until today. When an Indian child is born, his caste becomes the mini-community by which he identifies himself in a vast, potentially frightening country. Members of his caste will usually give help if he is in trouble. If he has to travel far, other caste members will provide companionship, help him find somewhere to stay, and maybe even get him a job. His family and most of his close friends will be from the same caste, and – most importantly – so will his wife.

Many Indians also continue to work in the traditional professions of their caste, though a person's choice of work also depends on local circumstances. For instance, if a man from the priestly caste has several sons (in a village where there are already enough priests), some of them may have to find other work. One might become a civil servant or a lawyer; a second son might get a job in a local factory; and the third might not be able to find any work except as a poorly-paid agricultural labourer.

But however poor he is, a high-caste man is usually choosy about his profession. Only some jobs are considered suitable for him. The most ancient professions are the ones most closely associated with caste barriers, whereas modern professions do not have the same taboos. For instance, a high-caste man would not become a shoe-maker, and a low-caste man could not become a priest in a major temple – but both might be able to train as nuclear scientists.

Jobs in the civil service or in the legal profession are not only "modern" jobs, but they are also associated with a good wage, security, power and prestige. These things make them appealing to people from every caste. Work in a factory is less appealing, but it usually provides more security than agricultural labour, and – being relatively modern – does not carry the weight of a centuries-old association with the lower castes.

Agriculture is almost the only ancient profession open to members of any caste (though the very highest castes usually only get involved indirectly, by employing a manager and labourers). This is because agriculture has always been the most common and important source of work, and it would always have been impossible to limit the people working in it to only one or two castes.

Not quite everyone in India belongs to a caste. Although the caste system has embraced most of India's minority religions, including Islam, Sikhism and Christianity, there are some 53 million people who have resisted becoming part of the system. These are the country's tribals. Tribals are thought to be the most direct descendants of India's pre-Aryan population, and many of them live in remote areas, in much the same way as their ancestors did many thousands of years ago. A few still live as primitive "hunter-gatherers". They survive by hunting and gathering wild fruit and vegetables in the forest. They don't grow any kind of crops, nor keep any domesticated animals.

Some tribals live by the ancient method of "slash and burn" agriculture. They live in forests, cutting down and burning all the trees in a chosen area. Then they scatter seeds for maize, beans, peas, millet and oilseed in the ashes. The soil is fresh and fertile, and for a few years it gives quite good crops, but after a while it no longer yields good results. When that happens, the tribals move to another part of the forest, and start again.

A few tribes still live self-sufficiently and in complete isolation from the rest

Nadeshan is a member of the Irula tribe in southern India. He is handling a cobra, which is one of the most poisonous snakes in the world. He has caught it for its venom, which is used by hospitals to make an antidote to snake-bites.

of Indian society, but over the centuries many thousands of tribes have been assimilated into society, and this process is continuing. Sometimes this happens because forest land is running out (commonly, because the tribals themselves have destroyed so much of it). Often, members of the tribe begin to see the advantages of education and better agricultural methods. By participating in wider society, they can also join in local politics and gain further advantages, such as Government grants and loans. Tribals who want to break out of their isolation usually

This wiry old gentleman is from the Nari Kuruva tribe, known as "Kings of the Forest". He regularly goes to the local market to sell fox furs, herbal medicines, and the plastic beads which he has made into necklaces.

imitate the religious and social customs of their neighbours, and after a few generations they may become accepted into Hindu society as another caste, though usually they end up at the bottom of the caste pile, as the poorest and most despised group.

Since Independence, the Government of India has been trying to make Indian society fairer and more equal. The practice of treating groups of people as "untouchable" has been made illegal, and it is now common to refer to Untouchables as Harijans, which means "Children of God", and is the name given to them by the great pre-Independence leader, Mahatma Gandhi. Measures have been introduced to make it easier for Harijans and other low-caste people to move up in society. But for most of them the weight of poverty and caste oppression is too great to be shaken off easily. In traditional rural society, the high castes will sometimes fight ruthlessly to prevent their ancient rights from being violated.

However, most Indians (including the least privileged) continue to believe in and rely on the caste system. In a world that is tough and competitive, they believe it is better to fight in a group than as individuals. That is one of the reasons why, over the past thousand years or more, caste has been such a stable element in Indian society. It has enabled many kinds of people from different races and parts of the world, with different customs, different eating habits, different gods and different professions, to live and work together as one social system.

There are other things which have contributed to the country's sense of unity. One of these is the religion of Hinduism. Although India contains about 77 million Muslims, 18 million Christians, 15 million Sikhs, 5 million Buddhists, 3.5 million Jains and a few other religious groups, the vast majority are Hindus – about 582 million of them. Hindus believe in many different gods and goddesses, each with his or her own name and personality, and each representing one aspect of the only God, who is in everything and who has no name, no body, and no personality. Some of these gods are only worshipped in a localized area, but the most important gods are common to all India. Their stories were recorded in some of the oldest texts in the world, and in rural areas (where the majority of people cannot read) they have been handed down by word of mouth from generation to generation. Through these stories, the most isolated villagers have gained an idea of their immense nation, which was the setting for the gods' adventures and battles. This sense of the religious unity of India is still continually confirmed through the common practice of pilgrimage. In most villages there are likely to be one or two people who have been on a pilgrimage to some holy place – perhaps even to a religious centre many thousands of miles away.

Another thing which binds the people of India is the fact that, even today, more than seven-tenths of the people depend on farming for their living. Although recently cities have grown substantially, India is still primarily a country of villages – some 600,000 of them. Furthermore, the same geography which has to some extent protected India from external influences, has also given it a characteristic climate. It is, generally, a very hot climate in which there are distinct dry and wet seasons, regulating the farming year. During the dry season there might not be any rain for months. During the wet season, it rains almost every day, and the rain beats hard, soaking everything in seconds. These wet seasons are called "Monsoon seasons" after the powerful Monsoon winds which blow the rain clouds in from the ocean during the hottest months of the year.

For many millions of people in India today, work is much the same as it would have been several centuries

This relief carving of a cow being milked at Mahabalipuram in southern India is more than 1000 years old. Today, cows and buffaloes are still being milked by hand, in exactly the same way. Cattle are still considered to be sacred animals, just as they were under the seventh-century Pallava kings who commissioned the carving.

ago. Farming methods have hardly changed. The bullock cart and the potter's wheel of contemporary villages are almost identical with those used 4000 years ago. The *dhobi* washes clothes in the same way as his forefathers did, by beating the dirt out of them against a rock. Clay dolls produced in Bengal today are very similar to those excavated by archeologists from a 2000-year-old site. Other things haven't changed either: although it is the policy of the Indian Government that all children should receive some schooling, this aim is still far from being achieved, and thousands of children in India are working instead of going to school (just as children did in England in the nineteenth century). Many of these children work at home, helping their families in a loving and secure environment – but many millions work in appalling conditions, ten to 15 hours a day for a daily wage of about 15 or 20 pence. Millions of men and women work in "bonded labour" which means they have become a kind of slave, tied to their employer and paid barely enough to survive.

Yet, in some areas of work, India is among the leaders in the world. It has more trained scientists and technicians than almost any other country. It has one of the largest railway and bus networks, and some of the best universities. It is also one of the top ten manufacturing countries, and it exports goods all over the globe. The world of people at work in India spans many centuries.

THE WORK OF RELIGION

Raman describes how he organized the festival:
"We had engaged two specialists . . . who were in demand all over South India.
. . . The chariot must be ready for the procession at eight in the evening, and they
would have to begin their work at eleven in the morning. . . . I gave them an
advance of fifty rupees and noted down their indent: seven thousand yellow
chrysanthemums, four thousand of a certain green plant, two thousand red
oleanders, two hundred thin bamboos splintered according to their
specifications, which they'd loop around the pedestal of the God, working the
flowers into them, and seventeen bundles of banana fibres thinly torn off for
binding the flowers. In addition to these basic requirements they had asked for
a thousand roses, twenty measures of jasmine buds, and bouquets and
garlands ready-made to be strung according to their specifications. . . . We were
taking all the flower supplies coming into town that day, and the price of flowers
for common folk shot up."
(From R K Narayan, *The Man-Eater of Malgudi*, Heinemann, 1962)

Raman is the main character in a story by one of India's greatest living novelists, R. K. Narayan. Raman is a small printer in Malgudi, an imaginary place based on the South Indian town of Mysore, where Narayan himself lives and writes. Raman has a small workshop with a back-room, where he mixes the inks and prepares the metal letters on a board, ready for

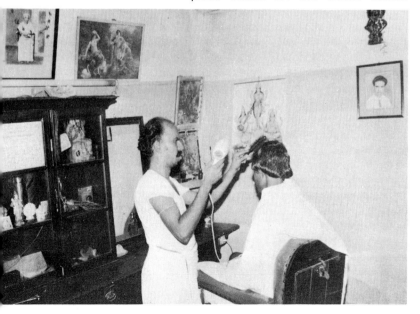

Traditionally, barbers in India have an important religious role. At every major stage in a child's religious life cycle, the barber is called to shave that child's head. He also regularly shaves the heads of pilgrims, or of any person who wants to offer his or her hair to the gods. This is often done as a form of thanksgiving if the god has granted some special boon, such as curing a person's illness. Barbers and their families are also often expected to play a major part in the arranging and organising of high-caste religious ceremonies – especially weddings.

Venkat, the barber in this picture, works in the city and no longer performs this kind of task (though he still shaves people's heads for religious ceremonies). He left his village when he was young because there was not enough work for him. At home, his father still fulfills the traditional religious role.

printing, and a front-room, where he receives his customers. But at the time of the story, he is organizing a huge religious festival to celebrate the completion of a long poem by one of the town's poets — one of Raman's customers. The poem is about the marriage of the god Krishna with the goddess Radha.

In India, religion is a central focus of everyday life. All kinds of daily actions such as getting up, washing and eating, are accompanied by some kind of mini-ritual. And every big event in a person's life is used as an occasion for a religious ceremony, or even a small festival (these are quite apart from the regular, annual religious festivals). Religion is a source of work for millions of people. Priests, astrologers, musicians, barbers, potters, cooks, flower vendors and all sorts of others are involved in the dispensing of religious ritual — and some make a great deal of money out of it.

THE FLOWER VENDOR

One of the most common ways of honouring the gods is by decorating their statues with flowers. Often, the honoured god or goddess is carried in a gorgeous chariot (also decorated with flowers) and paraded down the street in a procession. Even the poorest person will usually buy a small garland of flowers. In South India particularly, flowers can be bought on every city street corner, and in the villages, flower vendors often come on their bicycles carrying large baskets overflowing with garlands. They measure them against the length of their forearm, and sell them for a few pence per length.

THE FLOWER GARDENER

All sorts of other people make their living from the flower industry. There are the gardeners who grow them — either in small private plots, or as labourers on huge flower farms, growing roses, marigolds, and sweet-scented white jasmines of many varieties. Every day the flower buds are picked, with just enough stalk on the end to tie them into garlands. Then they are sold, either locally to small-time vendors, or to big merchants who transport and distribute them all over the country. Every day, plane-loads of fresh flower buds land in the major cities (especially in the southern state of Tamil Nadu), and are sold to hundreds of garland-makers. These men and women can be seen sitting on the pavements, or at large trestle

The author — who lived and worked in India for a year and a half — is buying a garland of sweet-smelling jasmine to put in her hair. On the right of the picture is a heap of loose flowers, and to the far right a pair of hands is tying the flowers together.

A young girl is making a rice-flour pattern on the doorstep of her home as a sign of welcome to Lakshmi, the Goddess of Prosperity.

tables, surrounded by baskets of loose flower buds which they skilfully make into long garlands, tying each flower with a string made from banana fibres.

Most of the daily religious rituals in a household are carried out by the women. They are the ones who clean and purify the house, and make beautiful rice-flour patterns outside the door to welcome Lakshmi, Goddess of Prosperity, into the home. They are also usually the ones who perform the daily *pujas* or ceremonies before the pictures of the gods hanging up on their walls. But for any major occasion, the services of religion "specialists" are required.

THE ASTROLOGER

The most important religion experts are the priest and the astrologer. Astrologers, like priests, usually learn their trade from their fathers and come from a specialist caste. There are astrologers to suit every pocket, and they are consulted every day by millions of people – from the humblest labourer to the most exalted film star or politician. Even Prime Minister Indira Gandhi (who died in 1984) used to consult one before announcing the date for the opening of Parliament.

When a child is born, one of the relatives notes down the exact time. The astrologer then studies the position of the stars and planets at that time, and draws up the child's horoscope or planetary chart. One of his most important tasks is to decide whether the horoscopes of two young people are compatible, and therefore whether it will be possible for them to

◄ Some of India's "religion experts" are extremely expensive. Others, like these roadside fortune tellers, charge very little. The "Astro-Palmist" (right) claims he can tell your past, present and future by looking at the lines and creases in the palm of your hand. The fortune teller (left) attracts attention with his green sacred parakeets. Each bird sits inside a cage beneath a picture of a god or goddess. For a few pence, you can choose one of the gods. The parakeet pops out of the cage, picks up a fortune card, and brings it to the fortune teller who reads it out to you.

▼

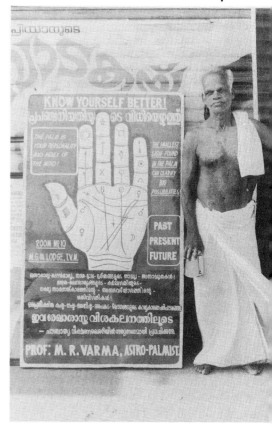

get married. But he is also consulted on all sorts of other questions. In the city, he might be asked to advise a businessman on where to make an investment, or whether to give someone a loan. In the countryside, he might be asked by a farmer to recommend an auspicious or lucky day on which to plough his field, sow his seeds, or sell his bullock.

THE PRIEST

A priest (on the right) is performing a "puja", or ceremony of homage, to the god. Two devotees have come to pay their respects.

Astrologers are normally consulted *before* any important decisions have been made – for advice. Priests are usually invited *after* the decision, to celebrate the occasion, and to ask for the gods' blessings on the venture. For instance, after a man has consulted an astrologer to decide when and how to build his new house,

he is likely to organize a ceremony to celebrate. If he can afford it, he invites his friends and relations to come. The priest burns incense and chants verses over a small sacred fire which he lights in front of the house. He breaks open a coconut and pours the sweet coconut milk over the doorstep, as an offering to the gods. The coconut is also blessed and offered to the gods, and the tender flesh is then scooped out of the shell and distributed to the guests. The priest blesses and distributes sacred ash, which the guests receive in the hollow of their left hand and smear over their foreheads with the fingers of the right hand.

Many ceremonies can be conducted without the help of a priest, who has to be paid, but a Hindu wedding is almost always a lavish occasion to which at least one priest is invited. The priests guide the engaged couple through a series of complicated rituals, and finally the ceremony reaches a climax when the groom places a special necklace round the neck of the bride, and they are married (the ritual is not quite the same in all parts of India).

THE BRAHMIN PRIEST

Not all Hindu wedding ceremonies are the same. They vary according to region, and according to caste. There are also many kinds of Hindu priests, specializing in the worship of different gods, and performing ceremonies for different castes. The highest and most respected kinds of priests are called Brahmins. From an early age, young Brahmins training for the priesthood are made to learn thousands of verses from ancient Hindu scriptures called the Vedas, which were first collected and memorized in about 1500 BC – more than 3000 years ago. The Vedas were written in a language called Sanskrit, which is no longer spoken by ordinary people today, and which even the majority of Brahmin priests do not understand. But Hindus believe that because the words are sacred, it is enough for a priest to chant them following the traditional ritual, for the ceremony to please the gods.

There have been Brahmins in India for thousands of years – at least since the time that the Vedas were written. In one of the later Vedic texts, society is describe as being divided into four main social groups or *varnas*. The highest *varna* is that of the Brahmins who are priests, scholars and teachers. The second highest *varna* is that of the Kshatriyas, who are rulers and warriors. (In practice, Brahmins and Kshatriyas were often competing for the top place in society, and it wasn't always clear who came out in the lead.) In third place come the Vaishyas, or traders, and finally the Shudras, who are cultivators. Untouchables (or Harijans) are a fifth group who are considered to be so low that they are not even included in the *varna* system. Theoretically, all of India's many hundreds of castes can be fitted into one of these five categories of people. In practice this neat division of society did not – and does not – correspond very well to real life.

BRAHMINS AT WORK OUTSIDE THE PRIESTHOOD

The *varna* system was probably invented by Brahmins who felt that as scholars and priests they deserved most respect, but nowadays there are many Brahmins who no longer believe that they are the highest-ranking group in society, and there are many more who no longer work as priests or have any detailed knowledge of the Sanskrit scriptures. Some work in agriculture, usually as landlords and managers, paying labourers to do the manual work. Others have become businessmen or civil servants. Brahmins who still live in the villages are more likely to have kept their high status in the local society and – as landlords – they are also likely to be wealthier than members of the other castes. Though they no longer work as priests, they are still expected to know more than the other castes do about Vedic scriptures, and they are also expected to be strict about behaving according to standards which are described as "pure" in the religious texts.

THE TEMPLE PRIEST

As well as performing ceremonies for high-caste individuals who need their services, Brahmin priests are in charge of looking after the gods and goddesses in the great Hindu temples dotted round India. Some of the larger temples are like mini-societies of Brahmins, in which different Brahmin castes are given different hereditary tasks to do. For instance, some of the priests are also cooks (only Brahmins are pure enough to be able to produce food which is fit to be offered to the gods – as well as to the high-caste people who come to the temple festivals). Other priests are gardeners, in charge of growing flowers for the gods inside the walled temple garden. Some of the priests are in charge of daily washing and oiling the bodies of the gods' statues, and then dressing them in clean clothes. Yet another group of priests wash these clothes – acting rather like priestly *dhobis*. Within the temple community, each Brahmin caste has a higher or a lower rank – just like the broader Indian society.

THE MUSICIAN

The large temples also employ many people from non-Brahmin castes, whose services are essential, but whose relatively polluting work gives them a lower status in society. Musicians for instance, are an essential part of many religious ceremonies, yet they are not considered to be very high-caste because their work involves putting the musical instrument repeatedly into their mouths, and stale saliva is thought to be polluting. Many musician castes have been traditionally attached to a temple, for which they are obliged to work a fixed number of days a month. In some temples they are paid in cash, but in most places their payment is in the form of temple lands which they are allowed to cultivate in return for their services. Many musicians also supplement their income by providing music for private religious occasions such as weddings, for which they get paid in cash.

THE LOW-CASTE PRIEST

Before Independence, Untouchables were forbidden from entering any of the great Hindu temples. Nowadays, it is illegal for any Hindu to be excluded from a temple, and temple-Brahmins have therefore been forced to perform *pujas* for anyone who comes in – including Harijans. But outside the great temples, most Brahmin priests still refuse to do any work for low-caste people. This means that in a community most castes – or groups of castes – have to have their own temples and their own priests or priestesses. (Among Brahmins only men can become priests, but the lower castes believe that women can also have special religious powers.) Low-caste people also worship their own local gods, as well as the major gods of Sanskrit literature. Their priests do not know any of the Sanskrit literature, and their ceremonies tend to be noisy, rowdy occasions, during which villagers often get possessed by a spirit and reel around in a trance until they collapse exhausted on the floor.

THE SHAMAN

Shamans, both male and female, are another kind of religion expert, making a living out of their speciality. They get possessed by spirits, like many ordinary villagers, but they are thought to have a special relationship with these spirits, and to understand them. For this reason, villagers consult them on many problems – from a bad harvest to the illness of a child. A Shaman often acts as a sort of village psychiatrist, helping disturbed and unhappy people to find some kind of peace.

In the rural areas, Shamans also often help to make ties between Hindu and non-Hindu communities (though usually mainly among the lower castes). This is because villagers – of whatever religion – often believe in the same local spirits, and therefore respect the same local Shamans.

THE AYURVEDIC DOCTOR

As well as the Shamans and other kinds of holy medicine-men, there are the sophisticated Ayurvedic doctors. Ayurvedic medicine, the Indian science of long life, is extremely ancient. The three most important texts on the subject were written in Sanskrit, and form a part of the holy Veda scriptures: they are the Ayur-Vedas, the Vedas which speak about health and the body.

Ayurvedic medicine is extremely complex and good Ayurvedic doctors have to train for years. They believe that being a doctor is not just about curing illnesses, but about promoting the physical and spiritual well-being of a person. A doctor must learn all about the patient so that he can advise him on a whole new way of healthy living. Unfortunately, many of the so-called Ayurvedic doctors who work in the Indian countryside know very little about this ancient science. In fact, they mainly use Western methods and drugs – even though they have not had any Western medical training.

This holy man dispenses both herbal medicines and religious wisdom to his customers.

THE SANYASSIN

Hindus believe in reincarnation. They think that life is like a kind of wheel which goes round and round, and that we are all born and reborn forever. Our life today is based on how good or bad we were in our previous life, and our future life will depend on our behaviour now. For most people, it is enough to live this life as well as possible. But Hindus also believe that it is possible for exceptionally holy people to escape the wheel of life, and to merge with God and the universe. For this reason, some Indians abandon their homes, their families, their castes, their ordinary way of life, and become Sanyassins, or holy men, devoting their entire lives to a search for God - the one, universal God, of which all the many gods and goddesses are just manifestations.

A Sanyassin does not work, in the ordinary sense. He lives by begging and usually doesn't have a home but wanders around from place to place, accepting hospitality or sleeping in the open. He has very few possessions and sometimes doesn't even wear clothes. Unlike the priest, he does not perform religious ceremonies or participate in everyday religious life. And unlike the Shaman, he doesn't usually try to mediate between the world of spirits and that of men. His main aim in life is purely personal spiritual fulfilment. But although he has stepped out of society and out of the caste system, he is usually a highly respected figure. Most Indians – of whatever religion – admire the Sanyassin because he has made the search for holiness his work.

LIFE AND LABOUR
IN THE VILLAGES

"Farmers are the lynch-pin of the world, for they support all other workers who cannot till the soil."
(From *The Tirukkural*, written about 2000 years ago by the Tamil sage, Tiruvalluvar)

THE FARMER

Farmer Siva is using his two strong bullocks to pull large quantities of water out of a deep well which has been dug in the ground. The water is collected in a large, round leather sack which is lowered into the well by a rope.

Siva belongs to a low farmer caste. He only has two acres of land, but he also owns a large well which never runs out of water. He can irrigate about half an acre, and grow enough rice to feed himself and his small family for a few months. Every morning, before sunrise, he gets up to water his field while it is still cool, and after harnessing his two bullocks, he spends about two hours leading them backwards and forwards as they pull water out of the well and into the irrigation channels which will flood the field. As the sun is going down, he starts again. The young rice plants (or "paddy", as rice is called before it is cleaned and husked) have to stand in several inches of water to grow properly.

These women are weeding ▶ in a field of cotton. The male supervisor gets paid twice their daily wage.

The traditional wooden plough is still used throughout most of India. In this picture, one of the men is standing on the end of the plough to dig it deeper into the hard ground, while the other man is guiding the bullocks. The land here is particularly dry and barren, which also makes it more difficult to plough. In the foreground, a little girl from the village is going to fetch water for her mother.

◀

On the rest of his land Siva tries to grow a pulse crop like lentils or millet. Pulses don't fetch as much as rice in the local market, but they need less water to grow. When Monsoon rains have been plentiful, the crop grows well, and he can sell the surplus. In a bad year, the crop often withers. The stalks are then only good for cattle — and even for them, it is a poor, dry food. Some of Siva's neighbours (who have no irrigated land) often can't even afford to buy seed and fertilizer for a pulse crop. They leave the land fallow, and feed their cattle on the meagre scrub which grows on it.

Siva has more land than many of his low-caste neighbours, but it isn't enough to survive on. To earn extra money, he works as an agricultural labourer for a fixed daily wage.

Unfortunately, there are many others looking for work, and sometimes there isn't enough for everyone. When that happens, Siva feels depressed and might go out drinking — even though he knows he is spending the family's last rupees.

There are approximately 150 million landless labourers in India who have to survive entirely on what they can earn in someone else's field. In some parts of the country, they get paid as little as six or seven rupees a day — which is less than 50 pence. Women often get paid less than half the men's wages, even though their hours are longer and their labour is equally tiring. Furthermore, women have to work at home as well — cooking, cleaning, washing, collecting wood, and many other household tasks. They are usually the first to get up and the last to go to bed.

In the fields men and women traditionally do different work. Men are in charge of preparing the land. They make and repair the irrigation channels and the huge rain-water reservoirs which are found in many villages. They level and plough the fields, and dig in the fertilizer. Women are in charge of transplanting young paddy plants, and of weeding, spending back-breaking hours bent forwards in the sun. When the crop is fully grown, the men cut it down, and — if it is a grain crop — men and women usually thresh it together, separating the grain from the stalk.

Almost everywhere in India, ancient methods of agriculture are used. In some states (particulary in the Sikh-dominated state of Punjab and in the north-west in general), farmers with Government aid have joined together to buy tractors and other machinery. But this is still rare. In most villages "modernization" means putting a metal blade on a traditional wooden plough, or using new improved strains of seeds which produce more abundant crops.

However, there have been significant improvements. By giving loans and grants for the digging of new wells and of canals to divert water from the rivers, the Government has greatly increased the amount of land under irrigation. Greater use of modern fertilizers and the introduction of new seed-types have also made an enormous difference to the amount of food which India produces. Since Independence total annual food-grain production has more than trebled from 54.9 million tonnes to 151.5 million tonnes. This has meant that since the famine of 1943 which killed about 3 million people, India has not only had no other major famine, but has even become a food exporter.

For most people, this achievement has only made a small difference to day-to-day life. Although drought no longer means starvation, many villagers — especially women and children — are badly undernourished (experts think that about one-third of the rural population is affected by food shortages), and fall easy victim to disease.

The reason for this continuing undernourishment in spite of increased production is poverty. Landless labourers are simply not paid enough to feed their families adequately. If there is a major drought or disaster, the Government distributes free food to prevent a famine. But when things are normal, the labourer has to survive on his tiny wage. Although he produces more food, he can't afford to buy more of it for himself and his family.

The ploughing season is a good time of year for Siva. With his own plough and bullocks, he gets paid twice the ordinary agricultural wage, and with the extra money he can afford to buy seed and fertilizer. The hardest time of year is during the long hot summer when food provisions are low and there is little work to do in the fields. Then, the family eats less well and the children are not given their

daily ration of milk. Siva usually manages to get through the year without getting into debt, but many of the village landless are forced to borrow money from a landlord, from the toddy-shop owner (toddy is a popular alcoholic drink fermented from palm tree juice), or from some other local rich man. They usually pay an enormous interest rate on the loan, so that they often become increasingly indebted over the years.

Along India's enormous coastline, much of the land is very sandy and unsuitable for growing crops, so seaside villages are populated almost entirely by fishermen and their families. Fisherfolk are usually fairly low-caste and quite poor (fishing is considered to be polluting work because it involves the killing of animals). They go out to sea in small wooden rowing boats (the design depends on the area) and catch the fish in large rope nets which they have made themselves. They usually have to fish at night, and when the sea is rough, their work can be very dangerous. They have no equipment or radio broadcasts to tell them that a storm is approaching.

A POOR FARMER'S WIFE

The children are about to take a flock of goats to graze on the village's common land. Because there is very little grass on the barren soil, grazing takes a long time and it will be at least three or four hours before they return.

Siva's wife, Jayantha, has to work in the fields to supplement the family income. She gets up before sunrise, at about 4 a.m., and sweeps the front of her mud house, before sprinkling it with water (to keep the dust down) and drawing a simple rice-flour pattern outside the front door. Then, she washes at the well, pulling water up in a bucket and pouring it over herself and her clothes (in the villages, women soap themselves underneath their clothes, so that they never have to be naked). Only then is she "pure" enough to start the cooking. She boils some rice – if she has any – or some millet, and some sauce with a few vegetables. Occasionally she cooks a tiny bit of meat (only the highest castes are vegetarian), but she can't afford that often. To save time, the family eat the same thing for breakfast and lunch.

After she has fed her family, she swallows down some food herself and rushes to the fields. Often she has to walk about seven miles to another village where there is usually more work available. This is tiring, but she walks with a group of other women, and they all chatter and laugh on the way.

While Jayantha is away, Balu, her five-year-old son, goes to school. Ten-year-old Lakshmi stays behind to look after the cattle. Since Siva bought the bullocks, two years ago, her labour has been needed at home, and she has stopped going to school. She also looks after her three-year-old brother, Murugan, who has been unable to walk properly for about a year, since he was paralysed in one leg by polio. Everywhere she goes, she carries him on her hip.

After breakfast, Lakshmi takes the bullocks and five goats to graze on the village common land, and to drink from the village water tank. In summer, when the tank is dry, she has

In the villages there are no gas or electric cookers. Wealthy women may have more – and more beautiful – pots and pans, but even they have to light a fire under them. Women spend several hours a day crouched over the smoke, which is very bad for their eyes. In this picture, Jayantha is blowing through a pipe to encourage the embers of the fire.

Although in the cities streets are often very dirty, Indians are personally extremely clean. Most Indians have a bath at least once a day, and they also usually wash their clothes daily. If they are lucky, there is a river, stream or canal nearby in which they can do their washing and bathe, enjoying the coolness of the water.

to fetch water from the well. She also gathers leaves and grasses to supplement the animals' meagre diet.

After four or five hours in the fields, Jayantha and the women walk home to feed their husbands. In the afternoons, while some men return to work and others rest, the women are busy. The morning's pans are scrubbed with earth or ash and rinsed with water from the well. Some of the wealthier high-caste women have their own private well. But Jayantha has to wait her turn at the communal well used by most of the people from her caste. After the pans, she washes the family's clothes, beating them clean against the cement rim surrounding the well. In some lucky villages, there are rivers, or large irrigation canals in which people can easily bathe and wash. But in other areas, women sometimes have to walk a mile or more to fetch the household water. Yet washing-time, like the walk to work, is an opportunity for the women to chat and discuss their problems. Some of them are regularly beaten by their drunken husbands.

In the late afternoon, Jayantha cooks and serves the evening meal, before herself eating. The family goes to bed early, at about eight or nine o'clock. Although there is electricity in the village, and a few street lamps light up the high-caste areas, Jayantha's street is dark. She has a small, home-made oil lamp which she uses for washing-up, but it's a strain on the eyes and she likes to put it out as soon as possible.

Some of the wealthier families have brick houses with cement floors, but most of the houses in the village are made of mud, with mud floors which need regular upkeep. Once a week, Jayantha makes a mixture of mud, water and cow-dung (which binds the mixture together), and washes it over her floor. This prevents the mud from cracking or breaking, and absorbs the accumulated dust. The mud stove on which Jayantha cooks has to be regularly maintained in the same way.

Cleaning, preparing and storing food also takes up a lot of time. Spices need to be laid out to dry and later ground to a powder. One of the longest jobs is removing the husks from rice and other grains. In some areas there are mills where this can be done mechanically for a small sum, but Jayantha does it herself. She places the paddy grain inside a hollow in the mud floor of her house, and pounds it with a long rod which breaks the husk. Afterwards, the grain is cleaned or "winnowed". Jayantha uses a large, plaited straw scoop with which she gathers up some grain and throws it into the air, catching it in the scoop when it falls. As she does this, the husk and dust, which are lighter than the grain, get blown away. Sometimes Jayantha grinds the rice with a gigantic pestle and mortar, and makes special rice dumplings called *idlis*, or rice pancakes, called *dosas*. (In northern India women often spend many hours grinding wheat to make a special kind of flat, unleavened bread called *chapatti*).

Low-caste women often work much harder than their high-caste neighbours – but they also have more freedom and independence. High-caste women who do not go out to work never have money of their own, and rely completely on their husbands. Sometimes they are hardly allowed out (especially in the north and among Muslim women). It is a question of prestige for high-caste wealthy husbands to keep their wives as secluded as possible, and it is also important for the ritual purity of a high-caste family that they should employ others to do those necessary tasks which are considered polluting. For these reasons, high-caste families usually employ agricultural labourers on their land, and members of the service castes for polluting tasks, such as washing clothes.

27

THE SERVICE CASTES

Both the high-caste and the service-caste families consider themselves bound to each other in a special relationship which must not be broken by either side – this is called the *jajmani* relationship. The high-caste family must never employ another family of *dhobis* (washermen) or barbers, and the service family must never abandon its employer in search of better conditions. The employer family is also expected to help when times are hard. At its best, this system provides mutual security. At its worst it can lead to terrible exploitation of the poorer, weaker castes.

In the traditional *jajmani* relationship, the service-caste families are not paid in cash, but are given a certain proportion of their employers' grain harvests. However, it is now becoming common for service castes to work for money as well – by taking on new customers outside the *jajmani* relationship. Agricultural labourers also used to be paid in kind, but this is

High-caste women usually get a *dhobi* to do their washing for them. The *dhobi* also irons the clothes, using a heavy metal iron which he fills with burning coal for heat.

less frequent nowadays. In many areas, landlords are no longer growing food crops such as rice or wheat, but have started cultivating banana, sugar-cane, cotton, and other "cash crops" which cannot be eaten as the main part of anyone's diet. Even in areas where the landlord is growing a food crop, labourers are increasingly paid in cash (except during harvest time when it is still common for the landlords to share out part of the crop). As there is no shortage of workers, employers have found it more profitable to abandon old *jajmani* relationships, and to pay their labourers in cash. They no longer have any of the traditional obligations towards their labour-force. Each day they can decide exactly how many they need to employ – and each day, men like Siva don't know whether they will find work. On the other hand, landlords often like to maintain *jajmani* relationships with at least a few of their labourer families because this means they can call on them in an emergency.

THE ARTISAN CASTES

As well as the service-castes who perform servant-like tasks (such as *dhobis* and sweepers for example) there is another group of castes who have a traditional skill which is needed by other villagers: this group includes blacksmiths, potters, carpenters, rope-makers and other artisans. They too often have *jajmani* relations with their employers, but they tend to be more independent because their specialized skills are widely needed. Unlike labourers, they usually have *jajmani* relations with more than one employer family, and they exchange their products with anyone who will pay them – whatever their caste.

Within an area, there is usually a broad interchange of skills and knowledge which links villages and opens communities to a wider world. In Siva's village for instance, there are *dhobis*, sweepers, shoe-makers, and blacksmiths – but there are no barbers, carpenters, midwives or medicine men. However, in a nearby village, there are three families of barbers who provide their shaving, haircutting and religious services to villages in a radius of about 20 miles. Siva and his neighbours regularly have their hair cut by one of these barber families. Similarly, when Siva needed a plough, he travelled to another village where he knew a good carpenter. When his wife Jayantha

Artisans like this potter are using ancient skills to provide villagers with tools and implements which they need. Sankar produces the clay pots, bowls and cups used in daily life, as well as more special vessels needed for weddings and other rituals. He is also a skilled clay sculptor, making a variety of religious images and statues.

was pregnant, he travelled to yet another village to fetch the local midwife. And when his son, Murugan, fell ill with polio, he took him to the medicine-man, two miles away – but the medicine-man couldn't help, and the boy became paralysed in the leg.

THE DOCTOR Since Murugan's polio, Siva has forged another kind of link with the outside world – through the local Western-trained doctor. Dr Kumar has a surgery in a small town about ten miles away. He charges 5 rupees (about 30 pence) for a consultation, and often asks for extra to cover the costs of tests. He also prescribes drugs, which are expensive. Siva still uses the medicine-man – who is cheaper – for minor illness in the

An Indian nun is giving an injection to a village toddler. She works in a well-equipped modern hospital run by an order of Christian priests.

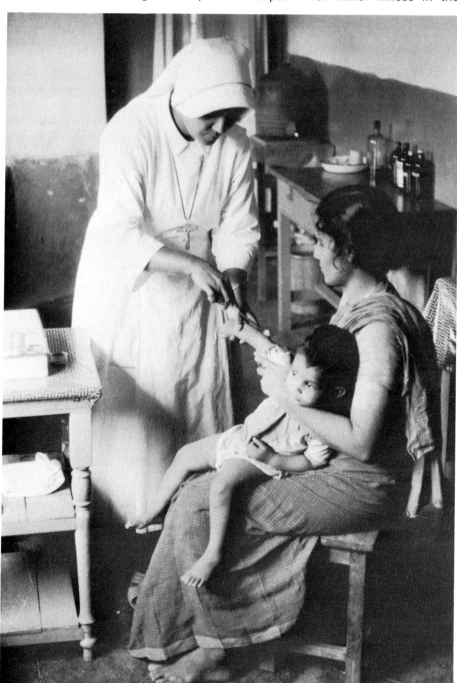

The surgery in this picture is largely funded by foreign agencies, but is run by Hindus. A female doctor is employed to examine the women patients.

family, but when Jayantha was weak with fever, he borrowed 100 rupees from an employer and took her to Dr Kumar. The doctor said Jayantha was severely anaemic because she had lost so much blood giving birth to her last baby, and she had continued getting weaker because her diet was too poor. He gave her iron injections and tablets, and eventually Jayantha got better.

India has many doctors qualified in Western-style medicine – some of whom work privately, like Dr Kumar, and some of whom work in Government hospitals, which are supposed to be free (in practice, poor people often have to pay bribes). There are also many hospitals run by charities, or often, by Christian nuns and priests. These usually provide good, free treatment, and are popular with the local populations. Doctors from such hospitals also travel round the villages giving hygiene and family planning training, and inoculating children against terrible diseases like polio and tuberculosis.

THE VILLAGE HEALTH WORKER

Finally, these Western-style doctors are often involved in the training of village health workers. They are usually ordinary villagers – men and women – who have volunteered and been selected to learn simple skills in medicine and hygiene. Once they are trained, the health workers are given a small salary to work among their own people, teaching them how to purify water by boiling it, and how to prevent children from dying of dehydration when they have diarrhoea. They also teach basic first aid, and go round making sure that sick patients take their pills regularly. This is a cheap and effective way of dealing with many of the health problems which villagers face.

Unfortunately, in spite of India's many qualified doctors, and numerous charity projects, the population is so huge and the problems of poverty so great that millions of Indians still do not have access to good medical facilities. For millions of villagers the greatest fear they have is that they will fall ill – for without their health they cannot work, and without working, they cannot support their families. There is no unemployment benefit in India.

THE WORLD BEYOND THE VILLAGE

What happened when the lorry came to the village:
"There was some commotion on the beach where a lorry had come and unloaded some timber. Now it was stuck in the sand. The driver was cursing loudly. Some of the village boys . . . came to help. They were spreading palm leaves on the sand under the wheels and trying to push the lorry out of the ruts onto them . . . the wheels churned and threw up sand, then the lorry heaved and roared and was on its way.
'Next time, send your timber in a bullock cart,' one of the boys shouted after the driver and they all hooted and laughed.
'You think I would drive a bullock cart?' the driver shouted at them from the window.
'Bullocks don't stick in the sand like your fancy motor,' they screamed, but he was gone."
(From Anita Desai, *The Village by the Sea*, Penguin 1985)

There are around 15 million bullock carts in India, forming the basis of the country's rural transport system. They link fields and villages to nearby towns and markets, and trudge to the cities where they mingle with the occasional camel cart (in the north), and with rickshaws, cars, trucks and buses. In spite of their slowness, bullock carts are popular because they are cheap and reliable, ideally suited to India's country roads.

Bullock carts often trudge slowly from villages to the cities, where they mingle with the city traffic. They are a slow but cheap and reliable form of transport.

TRADERS

One of the most popular forms of transport is the bicycle. Some 15 years ago, few people in the villages could afford one. Today, bicycles are used by thousands of people going to work – from ordinary labourers to office workers and even low-level bankers and businessmen. They are also used by farmers and artisans to carry their goods into market and for some small traders the bicycle is like a mobile shop. They pile their goods on the back, and ride round the villages selling anything from fruit and vegetables, to clothes and pots and pans. They perform a valuable service for those who are too poor or busy to travel frequently into town.

In towns and cities, mobile traders often display their goods on large trolleys which they wheel around.

Some sell sweets, biscuits and other kinds of snacks in the main shopping streets. Vegetable vendors and other food and household goods merchants usually push their trolleys on a fixed route down residential streets, calling at the homes of regular, middle-class customers. As they walk, they let out a distinctive holler to announce their arrival. In the early morning and evening, even the quietest street echoes with the cries of different vendors. The poorest traders simply walk around the streets (usually barefoot), or call in at people's houses carrying baskets of produce. Others set up shop on the pavement, spreading their wares on a piece of sackcloth or some newspapers.

Bicycles are often piled high with goods for sale.

Most shops are family businesses run from small premises (often tiny ones), overflowing with goods which are crammed into every inch of available space.

Indian cities are full of small open-fronted stores of every kind. Most shops are family businesses, and supermarkets are very rare. The most typical shop is the all-purpose store, which sells everything from rice to razorblades. Other stores specialize in selling just one kind of merchandise. For instance, some shops sell nothing but mattresses and cushions; others only have cloth or jewelry; and others are gleaming with stainless-steel pots, pans and plates. Whatever the shop, it is usually overflowing. Goods are stacked in precarious piles and strung

This young woman is selling cloves, cardamom, nutmeg and other spices which are extensively used in Indian cooking.

The shopkeeper is wearing a typical Muslim hat, but his shop is in a Hindu area, and his customers are almost all Hindu. The stainless-steel vessels in which Indians cook and eat are sold by the weight.

from the ceilings; shelves are crammed; even the floor is used for storage, with merchandise spilling over onto the pavement.

Some of the goods are made on the spot, by the shopkeepers themselves. At the back of the mattress shop, for instance, one can often see three or four men stitching and stuffing to produce the mattresses which are displayed in front. Most shopkeepers, however, get their merchandise from elsewhere. Sometimes, they get it direct from the producer — a local farmer or small manufacturer, but generally they buy from an intermediary or "middleman". Middlemen are also traders, but they don't have any shops or stalls. They make money by providing links between producers and other traders, all over India. They buy in one place and sell in another at a profit.

JOBS IN TRANSPORT

The volume of internal trade has increased enormously in recent times thanks to the rapid development of modern transport and communications. Today, Indian roads cover nearly a million miles, the railway system has grown into the fourth largest in the world, and the merchant shipping fleet is the biggest among developing countries.

On the highways, buses and lorries link with bullock carts and bicycles to carry goods and people all over the country. India's public bus service is cheap, extensive and generally efficient. There are also many private buses competing for routes and passengers, and keeping the price of travel down. Unfortunately, the standards of safety of these buses are sometimes equally low. Any businessman with money and contacts can get a licence to run a bus service, and though the vehicles are supposed to be checked for safety, nobody usually bothers. When they do, they can normally be bought off with a bribe. Brakes are often inadequate, and the suspension of the buses sometimes actually breaks under the weight of passengers.

Overloaded buses and lorries race at high speed, swaying dangerously down the nation's highways, their horns blaring to warn wandering cows, dogs, children and adults to get off the road. Drivers are often on the job for long hours, sometimes getting drunk, and even falling asleep at the wheel! (On the mountain road leading to the town of Ootacamund, in Tamil Nadu, there are signposts which warn: "Sleeping while driving is strictly prohibited.") Accidents are frequent. In Delhi alone, 348 people were killed and 2982 people were injured in buses during the 14 months before March 1987.

Although the road network is reaching out to more and more small villages, trains are still the country's primary means of transport. From a tiny beginning in April 1853, when the first train steamed off from Bombay to Thana (a stretch of 21 miles), the Indian railway network has gown into the fourth largest in the world, covering 38,412 miles, and running about 11,000 trains every day. In the last 30 years alone, passenger traffic has more than trebled, and today it is estimated that there are at least a million people travelling on the trains at any time during the day or night. In the year 1983 to 1984, they carried a staggering total of 3325 million passengers. During the same period they also carried 258,000 million tonnes of goods, supplying industries and traders throughout the country. About 1.5 million workers are regularly employed by the Indian railways, and a further 200,000 provide casual labour.

India is a large country and most train journeys last several hours, and some last several days. Poor people squeeze into tight spaces on the floor, under benches and on top of luggage racks. Ticket inspectors have a tough time picking their way through the crowds and checking every passenger. Whenever the train stops, the platform is suddenly filled with the sound of hawkers and the smells of sticky-sweet tea and coffee, and spicy Indian snacks.

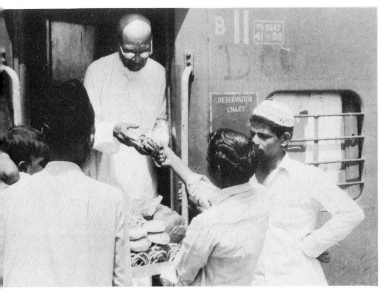

India's frequent and crowded trains provide an excellent ground for hawkers to ply their trade. They walk up and down the platform giving out their own special cries to attract the attention of passengers to the snacks, fruit, sweets and cigarettes which they are carrying on trays (like the vendor in the picture) or pushing about on trolleys.

For those who want something more substantial, the railway authorities employ cooks and caterers to provide cheap hot meals. Mid-morning and in the early evening, a couple of uniformed staff push through the carriages, taking orders. They then telegraph the order to the next station where cooks start working hurriedly. When the meals are piping hot, they are scooped into metal trays and rushed to the platform, in time for the arriving train. There is no need to provide cutlery since Indians traditionally eat with their fingers. When the passengers have finished, the trays are deposited at the next station where other railway employees pick them up and wash them in preparation for the next meal.

As well as travelling by road (in private cars – usually chauffeur-driven) and by train (first class), a small number of rich people use the internal airline system between India's major cities. For the high-powered business community in India – no less than for their colleagues in the West – the speed and efficiency of transport and communications is essential to success.

According to Indian Government statistics, more than 99 per cent of villages were receiving daily mail deliveries by March 1984. This claim may be a bit exaggerated, but considering the size of the country, and the inaccessibility of many of its villages, the Indian postal service is remarkably efficient. Mail is carried by surface and by air. Major cities are served directly by Indian airlines, and other cities, towns and villages are connected by all kinds of surface transport such as rail, road, boats, cycles, and – in parts of the North – camels and horses. At the end of the chain, the most common form of transport for the postman is the bicycle.

The telephone system is far less efficient. This is partly because demand among ordinary citizens is much smaller, partly because extreme weather conditions are constantly damaging the equipment, and partly because of the expense of setting up a modern and extensive telecommunications network. Though India has many technicians and engineers capable of setting one up, the Government has decided to spread the cost of doing so over a long period, so that every year the system is expanded and improved a little, but in the meantime it works very badly.

For most people, the state of the telephone network is irrelevant. In the villages practically no one needs or can afford a telephone, and even in the cities, only a minority of private households have their own hand-set. But for the country's businesses, not to mention its hospitals and Government departments, the time wasted through bad telephone communications can have serious consequences. It affects their own efficiency, and may be one of the main factors slowing down the economy's

Telephone engineers are a common sight in the city streets – especially during and just after the Monsoon season. Lashing winds and rains regularly damage hundred and thousands of telephone lines. The engineer on the right has taken a telephone out into the street in order to check an underground line.

growth. It also means that even a relatively small business has to employ its own telephonist, working to get connections through a jungle of telephone wires.

The Departments of Posts and Telecommunications together form one of India's largest employers. As with the railways, there are numerous administrators and clerical support staff. There are also scientific researchers, designers, manufacturers, technicians, switchboard operators and other kinds of telephonists; there are also the thousands of telephone repair engineers. These men can often be seen perched on the top of telephone poles, or crouched in the streets, fiddling with wires.

In the post and telegraph offices there are crowds, and chaotic queues. Posting letters and parcels often takes a long time. Standard airletters (which are a fixed weight and already have the stamp incorporated in them) can simply be pushed through the postbox but it is unwise to post any other mail without first having had it franked – to prevent the stamp from being stolen. Several queues have to be gone through to achieve this, and most businesses employ somebody especially to buy stamps and post letters.

In a corner of the post office, there is usually another queue for the telephone. Many city people wait hours for their call while the telephonist juggles with five or six numbers at once, hoping to get through to at least one of them. In yet another corner the telegraphist sits, tapping out messages by Morse code. Most Indian telegraphists are incredibly speedy, but however fast they work, they cannot get the text across as fast as on a modern Telex machine. Only a few of the largest post offices in the major cities have Telex machines, however.

BUSINESS AND INDUSTRY

A few of India's businessmen are multi-millionaires, owning giant industrial conglomerates, and exporting large quantities of raw materials and manufactured goods to countries all over the world. For them, work is very similar to that of their counterparts in the West. They have their own Telex machines, and frequently their own planes as well. For the freighting of export goods they either use one of India's 43 shipping lines, or – for perishable goods such as bananas – Air India, or some other major international airline.

By far the biggest of these

The man in the background is making a sari on his loom, while the girls in the foreground are spinning the thread for the cloth.

conglomerates are owned by two famous families – the Tatas and the Birlas. The Tatas are mainly involved in producing steel, trucks, power and chemicals, while the Birlas dominate in textiles, aluminium, cars and paper. Every year, they spend millions of dollars investing in new projects and setting up modern factories and plants.

Until recently, India's exports were dominated by farming products such as tea, sugar and cotton, raw materials such as iron ore, and semi-finished products such as thread and fabrics. Today, India not only manufactures almost everything for itself – from pins, stationery and fertilizers to steel, computers and supersonic fighters – but it has actually improved quality to such an extent that manufacturing now accounts for most of its exports as well. In 1980 manufactured goods were already accounting for 62 per cent of India's exports (up from 45 per cent in the 1960s), and engineering goods, now one of the biggest exports, earned the country one billion dollars (about £625 million) in 1981-2. At home, the recent substantial growth of the middle classes has also done much to boost the country's manufacturing industries. For instance, India now produces 600,000 fridges per year – four times more than it did ten years ago. Car production has more than doubled in the last five years to around 90,000 per year, and – amazingly – India is now the largest market in the world for two-wheelers such as motorcycles, scooters and mopeds. It has even become one of the major world markets for television and video sets. Although only a tiny minority can afford them, India is so huge that this amounts to a lot of people. In 1985 there were a million video sets in India – compared with 5 million in the United States just two years before.

In spite of these developments, the manufacture of fabrics remains the largest single industry in the country, the second source of employment after agriculture, and one of the major sources of exports (in 1980, textiles accounted for 20 per cent of India's total exports). About 40 per cent of fabrics are produced in textile mills using more-or-less modern machinery. The rest – about 3000 million metres of cloth a year – is produced on old-fashioned handlooms which have changed little since the seventh century BC, when India was exporting hand-woven cotton cloth to the Persian empire.

Weavers often work at home, or in Government-funded cooperatives. They produce cloth by the yard, or in the form of standard-sized *dhotis* and intricately bordered *saris*, sometimes edged with gold. Each region has its traditional patterns and special techniques. For instance, in the state of Andhra Pradesh, handloom weavers use an ancient tie-and-dye method which is one of the most difficult weaving processes in the world.

The Indian textile industry was severely damaged in the late eighteenth and nineteenth centuries, when the British began to block exports of Indian cloth in order to promote their *own* growing textile industry. In many areas, such as

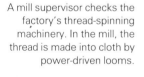

A mill supervisor checks the factory's thread-spinning machinery. In the mill, the thread is made into cloth by power-driven looms.

The woman is rolling a special kind of cheap Indian cigarette. *Bidis* are made of dried eucalyptus leaf, rolled around a sprinkling of tobacco and tied with a characteristic piece of pink string. She is working in a cooperative funded by foreign aid, and she receives 15 rupees a day (about £1) for her work. Most *bidi*-makers in the area work on piece rate for a private employer, and receive about five rupees for roughly the same amount of work.

lot of people but not much money, at the expense of more modern, automated industries. Consequently, a lot of things which are produced with sophisticated machinery in the West, are still made by hand in India. Some of industries sponsored by the Government are ancient rural crafts like basket weaving or the making of woollen carpets — which are hand-knotted in northern India. Others are hand-operated tech-nologies for the production of relatively modern goods such as matches, soap, and Indian-style cigarettes or *bidis*.

Many of these industries employ large numbers of people, but often in appalling conditions and at terrible rates of pay. For instance, match and firework factories in the southern state of Tamil Nadu employ about 100,000 people, including some 45,000 children. These children — aged between four and 15 — are woken by factory-agents at between three and five o'clock every morning. They are packed into buses and driven to work, where they labour for between ten and 15 hours a day, in return for a daily wage of between four and 20 pence — depending on their age and the speed of their work. Unlike regular factory workers, these children and their parents are rarely given secure employment with a fixed salary, or any other benefits such as sick-pay and retirement pensions. They are usually paid a "piece rate", which means they receive a certain sum for every piece they produce. But in spite of the bad pay and insecurity, and

Bengal, the local economy has never properly recovered, but since Independence the Indian Government has done a lot to encourage the industry once more, concentrating particularly on the promotion of handlooms. Unlike mills, handlooms are labour-intensive — meaning that more people have jobs — cheap to set up, and don't consume expensive energy.

Because India has a huge labour-force and little spare capital, it has been the Government's general policy to promote industries which require a although the work is often bad for the eyesight and extremely tedious, most people working in these industries feel grateful they have a job at all. In a total working population of about 300 million people or more, only about 23 million are lucky enough to have a job with protection from a trade union and such benefits as go with it.

Women and children, as well as men, are also commonly employed in back-breaking manual labour in the quarries and on the roads. Chunk by chunk, entire rock-faces are carved away by men with pickaxes. The women carry the large, heavy slabs to another part of the site where more women and children sit for hours in the boiling sun, breaking the rock into ever smaller pieces. Finally the rubble is mixed with tar and spread on the ground to create a road surface.

Many of the workers on these sites are bonded labourers – a kind of slave. Officially, bonded labour is illegal in India, but it is still widespread in industries such as quarrying, brick-making and farming, where plentiful and cheap labour are required. Poverty and unemployment continue regularly to push poor people into debt, and from debt to bonded labour. Often they are tricked into recruitment by middlemen who promise attractive wages and pay large sums in advance. The debt, with accumulated interest, becomes too heavy for the labourers to shake off. In this way they become enslaved to their employer, who feeds and clothes them, but ceases to pay them a wage. This kind of debt-bondage is hereditary, so a man's children are obliged to pay off their father's debt, even after he has died. And when *they* die, their children will be in bondage after them.

LIFE AND LABOUR
IN THE CITIES

What happened when the village boy went to the city:
"Hari went to work in the small kitchen at the back of the eating house. He saw there was nothing to scour the pots with except some blackened coconut husks and the ash from the fires, and he did the best he could. . . . They built up the fires, and then while one rolled out the *chapattis*, the other baked them over the fire with a pair of long tongs, and Hari was given the task of carrying them out to the customers eating at the long tables in the front room. There was so much work and such heat in that small place that no one ever seemed to have the strength or the time to talk. Hari too fell silent."
(From Anita Desai, *The Village by the Sea*, Penguin 1985)

Anita Desai's novel, *The Village by the Sea*, is based on the true story of a very poor family living in a fishing village on the western coast of India, near the big city of Bombay. The boy Hari cannot find work at home, and finally decides to try his fortune in Bombay. At first the city terrifies him with its noise, traffic and brutality. But Hari is lucky. Although the Sri Krishna Eating House (where he eventually finds work) is "the meanest and shabbiest restaurant" he has ever seen; although the work is hard and the hours are long; although he is alone with nowhere to sleep but the park in the summer and the eating house itself during the rainy season — in spite of all this, Hari is lucky because he has a regular job with a kind employer. He also finds a friend and protector in the old watch-mender next door, who takes him on as an apprentice and teaches him his trade. By the time Hari goes back to his village, he has learnt a new skill and has saved up enough to buy a few chickens for the chicken farm he is hoping to set up.

Every year thousands of people like Hari are drawn to the magnet of India's major cities — Delhi, Bombay, Calcutta and Madras — as well as to many smaller ones. Between 1975 and 1985 the population of India's cities went up by more than 45 million, and every fourth Indian now lives in a city or town. In Bombay alone it is estimated that 300 families arrive every day in search of work. For all those who are landless, unemployed, or whose land is so infertile that they can barely scrape a living from it, the cities seem to be busy, thriving places where anybody can become rich. The reality is usually very different. The pressure of population is so great that a one-room slum hut in the suburbs of the city can cost as much as £2000 — even though the few toilets that exist nearby are filthy, the garbage is hardly ever collected, and there is only one water pipe for every 20 or 30 households. Families of ten or fifteen people live in these single-room huts made of old planks of wood and corrugated-iron which absorb the sun's heat in the dry season, and let in the rains in the Monsoon, drenching their inhabitants for weeks on end.

Slum homes in the suburbs of Bombay.

Yet these slum-dwellers are not the city's poorest inhabitants. Some of them are Government and municipal workers (more than a fifth of Bombay's Municipal Corporation employees are thought to live in slums). Others are traders, and other kinds of small businessmen such as the owner of the Sri Krishna Eating House where Hari finds a job. They are not the poorest — but they cannot possibly afford the £100,000 or more which they would have to pay for a proper flat.

There are about 4.5 million people living in slums in Bombay. In Calcutta, conditions are even worse. About two-thirds of the city's 10.2 million people live in makeshift buildings, and over 300,000 live entirely on the pavements. Sanitary conditions in the city are so bad that more than 7000 people die in Calcutta every year from diseases such as dysentery, diarrhoea, tuberculosis and respiratory infections. In some slums, conditions are made even worse by the rule of the so-called "slum-lords". These gangsters have control over a band of thugs, and make a living by running a Mafia-style protection racket in which they extort rents and "safety money" from all the slum-dwellers who live or settle within a certain area.

In spite of these conditions, villagers continue to crowd into the cities, and only very rarely go back. A few move regularly between the city and country following seasonal work patterns (to the country during harvest time; to the city in search of casual labour during the rest of the year). But the majority prefer to stay put. Though disease is rampant, and infant mortality is even higher in the city slums than it is in the rural areas, for those who survive there are compensations. Rates of pay are normally higher than they are in the rural areas, and even for those who can't find a job (either as regular employees or as casual labourers), there are plenty of opportunities for self-employment.

CASUAL LABOURERS

Many of those who come to the cities start off as "coolies", carrying heavy loads in exchange for a few pence. At shipping yards, or in bus and railway stations, boys and men congregate in large numbers in the hope of finding some work. Whenever they see a ship coming in to be unloaded, or a passenger stepping out of a train laden with luggage, they rush forwards, pushing and competing to carry whatever they can. Young boys

43

"Coolies" like these carry heavy loads for others in return for a few pence.

are especially good at this as they slip easily between the crush and get at the work first. Grown men, on the other hand, can carry heavier loads and get paid more for the work they do. On a good day they might make 30 or 40 rupees (about £2 to £3), which is a good deal more than they would earn as agricultural labourers.

Some of the boys who have come to the city alone (like Hari) soon get caught up in begging and thieving rackets in which they are "employed" and "protected" by an adult who collects their day's takings, and gives them food and a few rupees in exchange. A few unlucky children are even mutilated by their patrons (they might have their tongues cut out or their limbs broken) so that they can collect more money from compassionate passers-by.

THE COBBLER In the cities, caste matters less than in the country. People from all castes are forced to mingle together, sit next to each other, and even touch each other when caught in a crush. But although increasing urbanization is beginning to break down some caste barriers, it is still very rare – even in cities – for young people to marry outside their own caste. There also remain certain kinds of work which only members of the very lowest castes will do. Shoemaking or mending, for instance, is exclusively an Untouchable profession – in the cities quite as much as in the countryside. Occasionally shoemakers have their own small shop or stall, but mostly they squat on the pavements and work there, stitching and glueing leather and rubber. For their repairs they use anything from old tyres, to reclaimed bits of leather from discarded shoes and sandals.

THE RAG-PICKER

"Rag-picking" is another strategy for survival adopted by some of the very poorest and lowest castes. This work is usually done by women and children, and it involves sifting through the city's rubbish, looking for any odds and ends that could be sold at a small profit. Old bottles, razorblades, scraps of metal and bits of paper – all these items, discarded by the richer middle classes, are collected, sold, re-used and re-processed by the poor. Bottles are cleaned and refilled; scraps of metal arè melted down; paper is put through the paper mill. In India almost nothing is wasted. Though rubbish is rarely collected officially, most of it disappears. Straying cows and goats eat a large part of it. The rest is collected by the rag-pickers, or burned.

For those who can't make a living any other way, begging in the streets of the city is a kind of work.

A rag-picker at work.

INDUSTRIAL WORKERS

For many it is the possibility of getting a regular and comparatively secure factory job which lures them away from the countryside. Between 1975 and 1985, factory employment shot up by about 40 per cent, and most of India's factories are based in the cities. In practice however, factory workers still form only a tiny percentage of the working population. It was estimated that there were only about 7 million regular factory workers in the whole of

Women and children are often employed on building sites to do the heavy work of carrying.

India in 1982. Many hopeful new-comers are therefore forced to find some other kind of employment.

One of the main sources of work in India's growing cities, is on the building sites, where everything is done by hand. Women are commonly employed to do the heavy work of carrying. They trudge backwards and forwards with a few bricks or a basket of sand on their heads. Using a spade, the men mix sand with water and cement to make concrete for the building. When the building has reached a certain height, scaffolding is made out of long tree branches tied together with rope. Men and women climb onto the scaffolding, stopping at different heights in order to form a kind of human ladder or pulley. Things are handed in small baskets and buckets from person to person, until they reach the top.

SELF-EMPLOYED WORKERS: THE RICKSHAW DRIVER AND THE TAXI DRIVER

Cycle-rickshaws are often badly oiled and in poor condition. It can be a difficult job cycling up a slope with a well-padded customer in the back. In such circumstances it is easier to pull.

For those who have managed to save a bit of money, the city offers other opportunities. Buying a rickshaw is one of the most popular ways of securing a better standard of living. The lowliest and cheapest kind of rickshaw is the cycle-rickshaw. These can be seen all over the city, ridden by wiry men, carrying fatter, flabbier passengers (putting on weight is a welcome sign of prosperity for all but the most Westernized of Indians). In the mornings and evenings, the rickshaws are suddenly overladen with crowds of neatly turned-out schoolchildren, black hair oiled and plaited, bright school uniforms crisp and freshly laundered. Parents usually hire a rickshaw to ferry their children on a regular basis.

A ride on a cycle-rickshaw costs one or two rupees. For those who want something speedier, but not as expensive as a taxi, there are the

"auto-rickshaws". An "auto" is a kind of three-wheeled scooter with two seats in the back, and canvas awning over the top. A ride in one of them can cost between five and 40 rupees (about 30p to £2.60), depending on the distance, and an auto driver can make a comparatively comfortable living.

The aristocrats of the city's private transport system are the taxi drivers. Sometimes their cars are 15 or 20 years old, and seem to be falling apart with rust. But the owners, unabashed, chase around the city racing against other taxi drivers in an attempt to establish superiority. In this job, as in many others in India, intense competition means that it is the toughest and quickest who survive.

Only two or three kinds of car are commonly seen in the streets of India, and they are all home-produced. This is because it has been the Govern-ment's policy since Independence to place an extremely heavy tax on foreign cars in order to promote the local car industry, thus employing more people to make them. The most common kind of car is called the Ambassador, and is a model based on the 1954 Morris Oxford. Although it is a cumbersome and old-fashioned car which guzzles petrol, it is in many ways ideally suited to Indian conditions — strong, reliable, long-lasting, comfortable on bumpy roads, and good in a crash. But because Ambassadors cost such a lot of money (at £4,850 in 1982, they were ex-pensive cars even by English standards), most car-owners in India keep their vehicle for many years, until they finally collapse. For this reason, although only a small minority of the population own cars, there is always plenty of work for car mechanics to do.

SKILLED TRADES-MEN: THE GARAGE MECHANIC, THE TAILOR AND THE TECHNICIAN

Most garage mechanics learn their trade at a very young age. It is common to see boys of six or seven, faces and arms blackened with motor oil, wielding spanners and screw-drivers. Other skilled trades, such as tailoring, are also commonly learned young. A tailor apprentice is first taught simple stitching, and only slowly graduates to more complicated

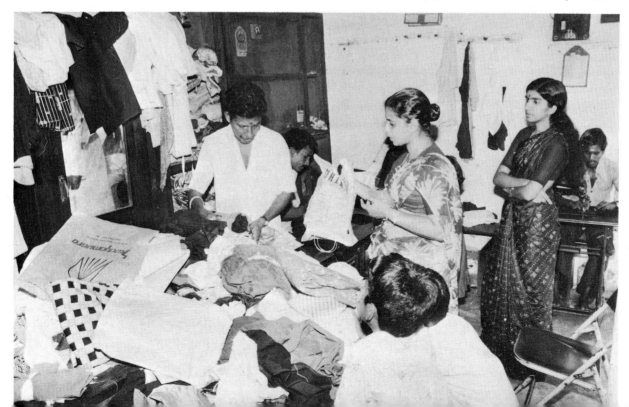

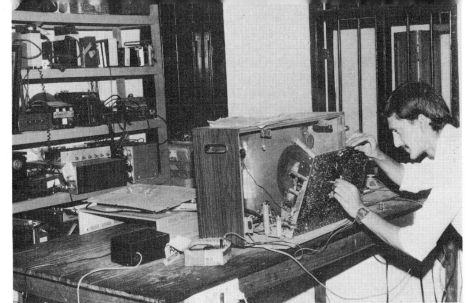

Paul Urban Henry's workshop.

Outside the electronic repairs shop.

◀ Appukuttam works as a tailor in the prosperous city of Trivandrum, in Kerala, south India. He began in the trade at the age of seven. Now he has his own workshop with four sewing machines and seven employees, all male.

tasks such as measuring and cutting. He is rarely paid a fixed salary, but receives a commission on every article that he stitches. At first, he will make only a few rupees a day, but for a young city boy, the simple opportunity of learning a skill is extremely valuable. A good tailor will never be short of work because in India people rarely buy factory-made clothes, and an ambitious apprentice aims to save up enough money to buy his own sewing machine and set up his own small business.

Although India is a poor country in which machines don't play as important a part as they do in the West, things are beginning to change. Not only are big businesses producing sophisticated equipment such as computers, but more and more small engineering and electronics workshops are being set up in the cities by enterprising individuals. One such shop was set up about ten years ago by a young Christian graduate from the state of Kerala, Paul Urban Henry. Paul is now in his early thirties. His workshop repairs all sorts of things, from toys and musical instruments, to radios, televisions, videos, cameras, and even computers. He has four employees (all Hindu, because – he says – they are better educated in this area), and a turnover of about 8000 rupees a month (about £532). His two junior staff receive a fixed monthly salary of 500 rupees (about £32), and the other two receive a share of the profits. He pays himself a salary of about 3000 rupees a month (£200), depending on the exact amount of profit he has made. His next ambition (which he hopes to achieve in about a year's time) is to become a distributor of T.V.s, videos and computers, buying from manufacturers at home and abroad, and selling to the local retail shops.

Skilled workers such as the tailor, the mechanic and the electronics technician are the aristocracy of the city's working class. Though they are not wealthy, they usually make a comfortable living. They can afford good food, clothing, and a few luxuries such as a watch, a radio, a bicycle, or maybe even a scooter. If they are not educated themselves, they usually make sure that their children are, and they probably have ambitions for them eventually to secure proper "white-collar" jobs as clerks, civil servants, or administrators in a large business.

THE WORK OF
THE PRIVILEGED

The Bachelor of Arts:
"Within six months of becoming a graduate Chandran began to receive suggestions from relatives and elderly friends of the family as to what he should do. . . . There was his mother's cousin who advised him to study Law. There was his Madras uncle who said that . . . he ought to go to the big city and see people. He himself volunteered to give a letter of introduction to some big man . . . who could in his turn give a further introduction to someone else, and finally fix up Chandran in the railways. This uncle seemed to live in an endless dream of introductory letters."
(From R.K. Narayan, *The Bachelor of Arts*, The University of Chicago Press, 1980)

Chandran is charming, intelligent and educated. But more importantly for his prospects, he is the son of a prosperous, high-caste retired District Judge. With a degree behind him, financial backing, and good contacts, Chandran is well-placed to get a job in almost any field. When he decides that he wants to become the "agent" in charge of expanding the sales of the *Daily Messenger* newspaper in his home town, he is introduced to the newspaper's management. He is immediately given the job, and the other applications are "filed".

THE ACADEMIC AND THE SCIENTIST

For the privileged, India is a country of great opportunities. While nearly two-thirds of the population cannot read or write, a tiny minority of the country's children are sent to exclusive public schools, some of which are only slightly Indianized versions of England's Eton and Harrow. There they are taught in English to a very high standard. Later, they can go to a vocational college, or become one of India's 3 million undergraduates in one of the 125 universities, where they continue to be taught in English. Many of the most brilliant students end up leaving India, and going to countries like America where they are paid a higher salary and are given more funds to pursue their research. By working away from home, they also enhance the prestige of Indian science abroad.

THE VILLAGE SCHOOLTEACHER

For the majority, however, education does not hold out great prospects. In most large villages there are free Government primary schools open to all, and there is usually a school within a few miles of the smaller hamlets. These schools are very basic, with just one classrooom, one schoolteacher and one class. Primary school children of all ages are taught together. During

School children often have their classes out of doors.

the summer they are usually taken out of doors and taught under the shade of a tree. During the Monsoon, they cram into the classroom.

When teachers are conscientious, these schools can give a reasonable service, providing children with the basics of reading, writing and arithmetic. Unfortunately, it is very difficult to attract good teachers into the rural areas. Most people with some education prefer to live in the cities, which are more prestigious, and where they receive a higher salary, as well as sometimes having the luxuries of running water and private toilets. In the country, teachers sometimes get paid as little as £12 or £15 a month. Consequently, many village teachers have barely completed the school curriculum themselves, and have had little, if any, kind of training.

Another problem in rural areas is that once children start becoming useful at home (looking after cattle, for instance), many parents stop sending them to school. Even if the school is

reasonably efficient, they don't feel its benefits outweigh the family's immediate need for extra labour. They know that at the end of years of schooling, the children may still remain agricultural labourers, like themselves. Today more than a third of the world's illiterates live in India. Although the Government has done a great deal to expand education, their efforts have not kept up with the population explosion. There are now 130 million more people who cannot read or write than there were at Independence.

In spite of this, education remains one of the best ways for poor people to break out of the centuries-old cycle of deprivation. In many villages there are at least one or two bright children of ambitious parents who have made it through school and university to a good job. These are usually children from higher castes, but occasionally a poor Untouchable child, helped by the Government's policy of positive discrimination, can also make it through the educational system.

On the blackboard:

HONESTY IS THE BEST POLICY

Tables and Mental Sums.

12-3-85

1. Mary had 14 sweets. She ate 5 sweets. Her mother gave her 6 more sweets. How many sweets does she have now?

2. How many necklaces can be made out of 48 beads, if each necklace is to have 8 beads?

...t of 40 pages of a book Mary ...d 34 pages. How many pages ...she yet to read?

$1 \times 16 =$
$15 \times 0 =$
$12 \times 6 =$

Mrs Mary Almeida is a Catholic, and works as a teacher in a Catholic school in Bombay. Like many fee-paying Christian schools, hers has a good academic reputation, and many Hindu parents send their children to it.

Because she works in a big city, Mrs Almeida receives the comparatively handsome teachers salary of Rs 1200, a month (about £80). Unlike many Government school teachers, she has a proper teaching qualification from a recognized teacher training college.

Whenever such a child becomes a university graduate, it is a source of great pride and encouragement for his entire community.

In the cities and small towns, the thirst for education is growing. For those who can afford it, there are alternatives to the low-standard Government schools. As well as the exclusive Eton-type public schools, there are increasing numbers of less expensive fee-paying schools run by private individuals or by religious organizations such as Hindu monasteries and Christian convents. Many of these schools are "English-medium" establishments, offering parents the prospect of propelling their children into the privileged Indian elite who can speak English. Some are merely profit-making ventures with very low standards, but many small schools offer a good service at a low price.

In recent years there has also been an increasing demand for further education, particularly for more technical, commercial and other vocational colleges (of which India now has many thousands). In the last ten years, for instance, the number of engineering colleges has doubled, while growing numbers of general colleges and universities have had to start evening classes and correspondence courses to cope with the need. In many of the newer, less prestigious, small-town colleges some 80 or 90 per cent of the students are now the children of parents who never went to college – a middle class in the making.

CLERICAL JOBS

Competition for jobs within this group is intense. Many find some kind of self-employment, either in commerce, or by hiring out their services on a freelance basis. For instance, some people invest in a table, a chair and a typewriter, and set themselves up as roadside secretaries. Some of the luckier, like Chandran, get jobs immediately, through contacts. But for those who do not have influential contacts or the financial backing to go into business, it can be extremely difficult to find a secure job with status to match their education. In June 1980, the employment exchanges had more than 7.5 million educated job-seekers on their books.

Administration is an important source of work for such people. The brightest pass the difficult Indian Civil Service examination and go into the rapid promotion stream of the central Government's administrative and diplomatic services. The less well-connected and educated end up as clerical workers and low-level officials. In Government offices, in banks, and in the administrative departments of large businesses, thousands of men and women are employed to handle the mountains of documents, letters and receipts spawned by the proliferating Indian bureaucracy.

The self-perpetuation of Indian bureaucracy leads to many terrible inefficiencies, but is difficult to suppress the 'red tape' because it fits in so well with the hierarchical nature of Indian society. Every bureaucrat, from the lowliest clerk to the highest official has his rank within the system. Each time the Indian bureaucrat stamps a document, tells someone to wait "a moment" (usually several hours) or insists on some lengthy procedure involving endless form-filling and letter-writing, he is showing his power and emphasizing his status.

There are other reasons why bureaucratic proliferation is so deeply ingrained. For the poorly paid official, insisting on lengthy procedure is sometimes the only way he has of earning a decent living. He relies on financial encouragement to increase his income, and in return for this he speeds up his work. Over the years, this kind of corruption has been spreading to higher and higher sections of Government service.

For the politician, the size of the bureaucracy is both a hindrance and an asset. He decries its inefficiencies when trying to achieve some political objective, yet he often uses his powers of patronage to push people into civil service jobs. In the urgent need to build a voting power-base for himself, the politician often invents new posts, which he then fills with his supporters. Tens of thousands of jobs have been created in this way, and procedural formalities have been expanded to fill the time of all these extra people. Much of the paperwork is done by hand.

As usual, it is poor people who suffer most from the inefficiencies of

Roadside typists set up shop next to hawkers and shoe-menders, selling their secretarial services to passers-by. They often type job application letters for students, or act as part-time secretaries to a few small businesses nearby. Sometimes they even act as translators, or help someone to compose a letter, as well as just typing it.

the system. Whereas the rich can afford to pay bribes, and the well-connected can get round many of the lengthy procedures, the poor often find themselves caught up in a thick web of bureaucracy in which their query or complaint is sometimes completely lost. Some of the saddest cases are those of children, picked up by the police for vagrancy, and then forgotten. An Indian journalist recently discovered that about 10 per cent of children taken into custody by the police in Bombay are kept in Government hostels for nine months or more before being returned to their parents, and hundreds are kept for several years. Many of these children have committed no crime other than that of being "of no fixed abode".

The fate of these children is similar to that of many thousands of so-called "undertrials". Arrested for a crime which they may or may not have committed, they are kept in jail until their trial. There, they may have to wait for years before their case comes before the courts — sometimes for longer than the maximum penalty they would have to serve if found guilty. Some of the people in jail are not even accused of having committed a crime — they are being kept as witnesses to someone else's crime. In 1985, the number of cases waiting to appear before the courts had risen to 10 million. In the Supreme Court (the highest court of appeal), it now takes at least five or six years before a case is heard, and it is common for judgments to be delivered as long as a year after the hearings are complete.

THE LAWYER One of the reasons for this paralysis of the courts is that there are not enough judges to cope with the work generated in such a vast country. Indian lawyers also tend to be long-winded. Whereas in America, lawyers present their arguments in writing, and in England they do so verbally, in India, lawyers do both. Behind the scenes, the problems are even greater. V. R. Krishna Iyer, a distinguished former Supreme Court judge, recently wrote an angry comment on the situation: "You will be scandalized to know that simple copies which a xerox machine will produce in a minute take one long year for a court to issue." He went on to complain of judges who arrived late and left early, and of days wasted on the formalities of adjourning cases and working out which judge should preside over which case in which court at which time, as well as endless other "silly causes paralysing public justice".

In spite of these huge problems, there have been some significant changes. The two most important developments were a result of the brilliant legal argument of a man who later became Chief Justice of the Supreme Court – Justice P.N. Bhagwati. In the 1970s he began to argue that it was the Government's duty to provide free legal aid. In 1980, it finally became the Government's policy to do so, and Bhagwati was made chairman of the newly formed Legal Aid Committee. Unfortunately this policy has not yet been made into law, so many of the country's state governments have not been very active in implementing it. None-theless, more than 284,000 people benefited from the committee in the three years between 1981 and 1984. This is tiny compared to the need, but it is a start.

Most importantly, Bhagwati successfully argued against a legal principle which said that only the person who had actually suffered a wrong was allowed to bring a case before the courts. This rule meant that poor, uneducated and illiterate people never had a chance of justice because they had neither the knowledge nor the money to go to court. When the rule was reversed, it became possible for any person or group to petition the courts on behalf on someone else. Since then, journalists, development groups and lawyers themselves have been very active in taking up these "public interest" cases, and have scored some notable successes. Pavement-dwellers, undertrials, inmates of mental homes, villagers who are victims of pollution, women forced into slavery, workers demanding the minimum wage – all these, and more, have been helped through public interest cases.

THE POLICE

In theory, India's police should be investigating cases where the strong have broken the law to exploit the weak. In practice, they are overworked, demoralized, and sometimes corrupt. Police constables are very badly paid, working an average of 10 to 12 hours a day (sometimes 14 or 15), six days a week – and often on Sundays as well. Their job is dangerous. Twenty-five per cent of policemen in service are injured at some time or other in their career, and the list of policemen killed on duty is becoming so large (more than 500 a year) that it cannot be read out at the annual commemoration parade because people get restless. In spite of all this, the prospects of promotion for the average policeman are tiny. More than three-quarters of the men retire at the rank to which they were recruited.

Although the number of policemen in India is well above a million, they are badly equipped and the problems they face are huge. India is a volatile country. Social tensions often erupt into violence. Occasionally clashes develop into riots in which dozens – sometimes hundreds – of people are killed. In October 1984, when Prime Minister Indira Gandhi was assassinated by a Sikh extremist, the people of Delhi went into a frenzy of communal rioting in which nearly 3000 innocent Sikh civilians were massacred. Many policemen stood by, watching the violence. It wasn't until the army was called out three days later that the situation was brought under control.

In response to India's violence, the police often use violent methods of control. Demonstrations are usually broken up with cane charges or gunfire (people are often killed in the process). Confessions are extracted with the help of a *lathi* (a kind of four-foot-long truncheon). Witnesses are often bullied into appearing before the courts, and if genuine witnesses can't be found, others are persuaded to testify. Sometimes, suspected criminals are "punished" by the police immediately, dispensing with the need for a trial. When evidence is so difficult to obtain, and the courts are so clogged up that it may be years before a case comes up, the police feel justified in using such methods. Though brutal, they produce results and are often supported by ordinary citizens.

In spite of this, the police are unpopular with the general public. Although there are some honest and idealistic policemen, many succumb to outside pressures and take bribes from the public to supplement their income. Pressures also come from politicians who expect the police not to obstruct them or their wealthy supporters, even when the law would require it. Because politicians need the good will and the money of local businessmen they will sometimes use their power to demote or transfer any policeman who stands in their way.

THE POLITICIAN

The cost of fighting elections is enormous. Most constituencies are huge, and parliamentary candidates need to spend enormous amounts just to get round them. They buy jeeps and loud speakers. They print posters and pay for canvassers. They buy hundreds of *dhotis* and *saris* which they donate to poor people as "good will gestures". They rent buses and buy huge quantities of beer and toddy, enticing large crowds of villagers to huge demonstrations in support of themselves and their party. In addition, some candidates (especially in the North) spend money on hiring gangs of thugs to terrorize opponents and capture voting booths, making it impossible for anyone to vote freely at that particular booth.

For these reasons, it is rare for a poor man to become an M.P. Although candidates are given substantial financial backing by their parties, they are not normally chosen as candidates at all unless they have money and contacts of their own. Once they have been elected, many politicians take advantage of their positions of power to accumulate more wealth.

Many Indians are depressed by this decline in public morality since Independence. Entire villages occasionally decide to boycott elections in protest. The press rages against corruption; top civil servants, lawyers, and a few politicians themselves engage in agonized soul-searching.

A few measures have been taken by the Central Government to improve this situation. For instance, during election times voters now have their thumbs marked with indelible ink to make sure they don't vote more than once (the ink wears away, but cannot be washed off). One of Rajiv Gandhi's first important acts as Prime Minister after his mother's assassination, was to pass an "anti-defection" law designed to prevent politicians from being bribed into switching from one party to another at whim. This measure has given a certain amount of stability to state government politics, and has prevented some of the more gross abuses of power. But

During election time every political party in India adopts a distinctive symbol by which illiterate people can recognize them. This city slum dweller is doing her washing under the Communist Party symbol.

change can only happen slowly. Even the most idealistic of politicians has to work within the flawed democratic system if he is to survive in politics at all.

THE NEWSPAPER JOURNALIST

One of the most encouraging developments for the health of India's democracy has been the growth of the press. Since the late 1970s, newspaper journalists have been increasing the scope of their reports. Today, they no longer confine themselves to recording the activities and pronouncements of the Government, but also attempt to explain and investigate the news. The new breed of investigative journalist has done much to expose social and political evils. The middle classes are now better informed than ever. The circulation of newspapers has grown to more than 40 million, and is continuing to expand. Traditionally, only the cream of India's society – the English speakers – regularly read newspapers, but in some areas today, the Indian-language press is growing even faster than the English press.

THE BROADCASTER

Radio and television have not developed with the same vigour. They are strictly controlled by the Government, and newspaper journalists often view their broadcasting colleagues with exasperation, accusing them of trying to please the authorities. Although the number of television sets is increasing (there are now 5.5 million of them), and soap operas are beginning to draw large crowds round the occasional village set, it is still a comparatively unimportant medium. Radio sets are much more common. They are one of the first luxuries people buy. In the villages it is common for at least one or two families to own one, and in the city streets, the radio is often broadcast on loudspeakers for all to hear. But the radio's popularity derives almost entirely from the film world. It is the sound of endless film songs which can be heard blaring down the streets – and which binds people from the North and South in a common passion.

Radios are one of the first luxuries poor people buy.

THE FILM STAR AND THE FILM STAR POLITICIAN

Indian films are almost always musicals. Demure young women and macho men suddenly break into song and raunchy disco dancing. But although the dancing can be quite suggestive, Indian films are actually very prudish. Even a kiss on the screen is considered to be extremely daring.

The Indian film industry is the largest in the world. Every year film-makers bring out more than 800 titles to satisfy the national hunger for romance, swashbuckling heroes and voluptuous heroines. Recently, the industry's profits have suffered from heavy taxation, and from illegally pirated videos (although very few people have their own video machines, they go to video parlours where they can see films at a fraction of the price they would have to pay in a cinema). But it is still film — more than any other medium — which has captured the imagination of the masses. Its influence on the public is probably greater than anywhere else in the world. Cinema halls are almost always packed out. Villagers regularly walk several miles to see the latest sensation showing at the nearest corrugated-iron shack which serves as a cinema. Actors and actresses are

elevated into Hollywood-style super-stars, with a following of millions of fans.

The influence of the cinema is so strong that politicians have been exploiting it increasingly. This trend was first started in the southern Indian state of Tamil Nadu, where local politicians began to campaign through films written, directed and acted by their own supporters. The strategy was immensely successful, and for the past 20 years or so, the Tamil political scene has been dominated by characters from the film world. M.G. Ramachandran, Chief Minister of the state until the end of 1987, was himself an elderly ex-film-star. His popularity was so immense that when he nearly died of a stroke in late 1984, the people of Tamil Nadu went into a state of near frenzy. Prayer meetings and huge marches were held evey day. Hundreds went on an

indefinite fast and thousands kept vigil outside his hospital in the city of Madras. More than 20 people even committed suicide, burning themselves to death in sympathy. When he finally died in December 1987, Tamil Nadu was thrown into such political turmoil that the Prime Minister, Rajiv Gandhi felt himself forced to impose central Governmental rule on the state in order to restore order.

For millions of villagers, the border between romance and reality blurs as they contemplate the unfamiliar worlds of politics and the cinema. They go to the cinema to find relief in fantasy from the toil of the fields. But for many, the glamour of the screen influences their perception and their hopes of life beyond the village. Though the world of work in India is still predominantly rural, things are changing very fast as the cities continue to swell. For the Government of India, this urban growth is a major problem. Work urgently needs to be taken back into the villages. Rural industries need to be promoted and expanded. Glamour has to be restored to the countryside.

GLOSSARY

Ayurvedic medicine   ancient Indian science of long life.

bidis   Indian-style cigarettes.

bonded labour   form of work in which employee is like a slave to the employer.

Brahmins   priests, scholars and teachers: the highest *varna*.

caste   Hindu hereditary class, with members socially equal, united in religion, and usually following the same trades.

chapatti   type of flat, unleavened bread.

coolies   men offering to carry heavy loads in return for payment.

dhobi   laundryman.

dhoti   white cloth wrapped round legs, worn by men in northern India.

dosa   rice pancake.

Harijans   another word for Untouchables, meaning "Children of God".

hunter-gatherers   people who survive by hunting animals and gathering fruit and vegetables.

iddli   rice dumpling.

Jains   members of the Jain religion, an offshoot of Hinduism which emerged in the sixth century as a reaction against the complicated rules of Brahminical religion.

jajmani   the special relationship between higher and lower castes, which binds them together.

Kshatriyas   kings and warriors: the second-highest *varna*.

lathi   four-foot-long truncheon used by Indian police.

lunghi   coloured cloth tied round stomach like skirt, worn by men in southern India.

Monsoon   rainy season accompanying wind from the south-west in summer.

puja   daily religious ceremony carried out inside the home.

rickshaw   bicycle used for carrying passengers.

Sanskrit   ancient and sacred language of the Hindus in India.

Sanyassins   holy men who devote their lives to God and live by begging.

sari   long piece of cloth worn as clothing by women.

Shamans   religion experts, thought to have a special relationship with the spirit world.

Shudras   cultivators: the fourth-highest *varna*.

tribals	descendants of India's oldest inhabitants; they are not members of the caste system.
slash and burn	form of agriculture involving the cutting down and burning of an area of forest, and the sowing of seeds in the ash-enriched soil.
undertrials	people kept in jail awaiting trial.
Untouchables	low-caste people considered by others to be "polluting".
Vaishyas	traders: the third highest *varna*.
varna	Hindu social grouping; there are four main *varnas*.
Vedas	ancient and sacred Hindu scriptures.

BOOK LIST

Durrans, Brian and Knox, Robert	*India: Past into Present*, British Museum, 1982
Fishlock, Trevor	*India File: Inside the Subcontinent*, John Murray, 1983
Narayan, R.K.	*The Painter of Signs*, Penguin, 1977
Watson, Francis	*A Concise History of India*, Thames and Hudson, 1979
Wiser, W.H. and C.V.	*Behind Mud Walls 1930-1960*, University of California Press, 1963
	Bhagavad Gita, translated by Juan Mascaro, Penguin, 1962
	Mahabharata, abridged by R.K. Narayan, Viking, 1978

ACKNOWLEDGMENTS

All the photographs were taken by John Ogle, except cover picture bottom right, taken by Naresh Sohal. The map on page 3 was drawn by R.F. Brien.

INDEX

30/-